AROUND THE GATE

Around the Gate

poems

M.A. Nicholson

For Christiani
Thank you for
your support,
io chi siamo

THE WORD WORKS
Washington, D. C.

The Word Works
P.O. Box 42164
Washington, D.C. 20015
editor@wordworksbooks.org

Cover art:
Cover design: Susan Pearce
Author photograph: Tori Green

ISBN: 978-1-944585-81-5

Acknowledgments

Thank you to the following publications, their editing staff and readers, for supporting my work and giving early iterations of some of these poems their first homes:

American Academy of Poets – "The Ballad of Double D"
Bear Review – "Cute, Joyce" and "Creole Recipe Card for
       Nonviolence"
Best New Poets 2022 – "Dandies, Wilde"
Ellipsis – "Radio Signal from ɑCMa," "Return from Thunder Rock,"
       and "The Ballad of Double D"
Peauxdunque Review – "Watching Uncle Pit's Place Burn" and
       "After the Twister"
Talking River Review – "Practicing off the Coast of Lido"
Tilted House Review – "Ariadne's Side" and "The River Merchant's Wife"
Trampoline Poetry – "Solstice Ritual With My First-Born"

Thank you to The Word Works. I am honored and delighted to be a part of your tradition and family.

Thank you to Carolyne Wright, for believing in my work and for giving me the opportunity to share it with the world.

Thank you to Brad Richard, for your time and careful attention as an editor and for your commitment to the literary arts and artists.

◊ ◊ ◊

I'd also like to express much love and immense gratitude to the many members of my family and community, who inspire and support me, and without whom this manuscript likely would not exist and certainly would not exist in this particular form:

To Carolyn Hembree, my treasured friend and mentor—whose courage and dedication embolden me as a poet, teacher, and human—for the countless hours of collaboration and guidance.

To Tori Green, my daughter and creative partner, my first true love—who has given me intellectual and creative inspiration and whose work as an art historian sparked many of these poems—for being my most dependable editor and for creating such gorgeous artwork, including the installation featured on the cover of this book.

To Alice Mae and Andrew Meza—who, through their words and actions, taught me the meaning of love, community, and home—for this inheritance, the gifts of memory and storytelling.

To my parents, sisters, aunts and uncles, and cousins—whose humor, tenacity, compassion, and generosity have served as my true north—for providing a lifetime of encouragement and support.

To Ethan Ballard, my fearless philosophizing son—whose capacity for patience, understanding, and love are unparalleled—for challenging me and my poetry so we may continue to grow.

To the folks of the Creative Writing Workshop at the University of New Orleans—who are relentless in their devotion to The Work and to our literary community, as a whole—for contributing their time, insight, and brilliance in the making this book.

To my readers and to all the other members of my family and community in New Orleans and beyond—many of whom are noted throughout the book but whose numbers are too vast to include in a single manuscript—for cocreating this reality. Truly, *io chi siamo*.

Contents

IV

V

for my city, my people, my family

◊
◊
◊

Not Whether but When the River Rises

how simple the miracle of a memory
of sky

      memory of stars, courtyard
      -framed

         sheltered from / light / in this city
      invisible / remembering / the swamp

        remembering
at its door / at its skirt / at the tip   of its tongue
                                    is a language
                                    not lost
                          but

      unuttered / felt / a steady
         strum

the vocals of / our river / resounding from
the amphitheater of / New Orleans / hallowed

                        acoustic / clap
                        of so many
                        feet over

cobble / over time / the city's
a voice in sync / with these harmonizing echoes / where the earth

                sinks / as it rises / the river's
                        wake
                    remembers
          it was more than once a flood

        ~ for DKL

On Chartres With Headless John the Baptist

Here is the Church.
Here is the Steeple.
Just open up
to see all the people.

Or our own hands
as they jot notes
cadenced by acid
jazz, etched grooves

traced on a blank
plane. Paper
worship is the same
as conversation or

change recovered
from a bar, the floor
between here and
there resisting

erasure to supply
the demand of thirsty
throats chasing
lyrics—like cane

in the brakes marking
fertile lands,
for carving ancient
reeds for fishing

or for bending
breath to herald—
welcoming, absorbing,
parting tidal

waves to drum
gently: a projection
to activate
your inner ear.

Just a few
notches, angled
and intersecting
incisions, may

pierce the woody
exterior, carve
a path for sweet
sap, what

green renders sunlight,
what green offers—
not a stalk,
but a staff,

to chew upon,
to suck dry,
to convert into
an instrument

delivering
sustenance:
delivering
song.

~ for CTS

Ars Poetica

Cyclically, the crawfish draws
backwards amongst cypress knees.
Splits its shell. Pushes its exo

-skeleton ahead. Burrowing,
hides its new body
behind—soft but still

moving strong sturdy.
If they ask, tell them this
is what I meant

even when I first began:
I luminate with intent to regress
and no presumption to end—so

when jasper-light retreats,
purpling windowpanes, when light casts
trailing shadows through magnolia canopies,

I grow in monochrome—
breathe in waves—
stir from dreams.

When questions whelm, I reveal
by reflecting. I keep time. I take time.
I take. Enough.

                    ~ for JG

Visiting Family at St. Roch Cemetery

Could steel resist his soft-press face of glass?
His mushroomed polka dots in oxford pleats?
Etched marble holds his visage in the past:
My uncle's crushing death was on repeat ...

If only his was clean, like guillotine—
or something fair, like drifting in his sleep.
Maw's kitchen towels grip her at the sink.
She dreams she could have stopped what was foreseen.

I dream of ways that I can break the scene ...
I run out back and to the window screen—
jump and wave my arms: *What do you see?*
Put on your shoes, come on—you go with me.

Our dead no longer stand around the gate.
You've done your work—there's no reason to wait.
Just take my hand and walk and wing with me—
remind me of the stories I must keep.

~ *for AMM*

Some Kind of Creole

Core. Lexical. Meaning. *from*

sounds　—Proto-Indo-European　[*ker- to become　bigger or　　to grow]

　　　　　　　　　　· noun (declines eight, nine times ...

　　　　　how do we say it? out
　　　　　loud

　　　　　　　　　　　　　　Beget. Be gets.　be—get

　　　　1. so many　cases
　　　　　　　　of ways

　　　　　　　　　to be raised in　　one's own
　　　　　　　　　　　　　　house

　　　　2. org. cop y right ed now heir loom kre
　　　　　　　　　　ole is a vine that sprawls
　　　　　　　　　　taps roots mult i
　　　　　　　　　　　　　　　　　　plies yields

　　　　　3. (in)determinate in
　　　　　　　　　　　　　　its native habitat
produces
　　　　　　　　plentiful
　　　　　　　　　　fruits

4. *a perennial vine*
　　　　　　　　　replants itself　　　*leaving nets*
　　　　of old-growth　　　　*behind*

　　　　　~ for MS

I Am Who We Are

A rotating fan.

My mother, eight months pregnant with my sister. The creak of her rocking chair. The amber glow of the circle of our lantern's shade.

There was no wall beyond the pressing dark, the pressing heat of our New Orleans home in spring. I was pulling at her knee,

pressing my forehead, my cheek, into sheer cotton. In her lap was the biggest bar of chocolate I'd ever seen.

She was rocking, shaking, weeping. The fan ticked, intermittent. Quiet heat. Muggy wind. Whir and pummel. Clinging. Too.

Uncle An gone. Daddy gone. Too.

The rocking slowed. She peeled back the wrapper, finally spoke

Would you like a piece?

with her eyes only. Her hand snapped off a corner. Her eyes looked toward mine again.

Yes—

I replied by standing up, reaching out my open hand.

◊

A chalkboard easel. Long parallel lines, divided by dashes.

My cousin Leslie was tall. We played Simon Says. Pretended to be cheerleaders. Jumped on her trampoline.

She had a slender wooden wand in her hand, pointing at shapes:
some straight lines, angles and arrows; some circles. She pointed
and I repeated *This letter's name is*

A ...   E ...   I ...

And O! how I leapt to my feet, clapped my hands together, when
I thought one of those letters was a secret code for *ME*.

~for LF

Maximum Velocity

My home, my neighborhood, remains—
the sidewalk where I first drove—

Big Kid on Strawberry Shortcake Power Wheels cruising
down Pauline Street to St. Claude—not keeping up but being

seen—a slow parallel with the highway—with
wagons, dusters, jalopies. I was light amidst heavy metal

flying past my tiny parade—foot pressing, pushing maximum velocity at
two years old, head held porch-high past pink azalea
blooms

all the way to the junk shop, where my mother would trade
with the Avon lady, rollers in her hair, blowing smoke that swirled

around innumerable treasures—
appliances stacked to the ceiling,

women's heads stooped together
in a dim lit corner store.

~ for DAM

Public Programming

1984, The World's Fair, glamorous, with gondolas crossing high
over the Mississippi—over the heads of so many as little as me;

1986, *The Challenger*, the Teacher in Space Project, blasting,
exploding common folk, teachers like mine, Ms. Rabelais;

1988, *The Secret Garden*, a wild-blossoming ordered by children
growing behind a wall and a locked door;

1989, newscasters repeating news—hot sun pouring into
our classroom windows—

as the television pitched night
from Berlin that day:

Men perched high on a wall—fireworks illuminated wide mouths,
faces, moving silhouettes, slippery windbreakers, fists—

shadows were the reason for not knowing
if they jeered or cheered.

Many more clamored below,
trying to climb.

Weeks later, I was told people could buy its broken bits—people
like my teacher who beamed when she repeated

This is history! passing her purchased artifact, student-to-student.
I took the box. Lifted the lid. Found it lying

on a bed of cotton. One side was rough concrete, the other
smooth and spray-painted: yellow, black, and green,

a shard of what could have been any sidewalk or driveway, it was
nearly weightless in hand.

A Gift of Onions

~after Osman Kalin's Treehouse on the Wall

The river Spree spliced East and West Berlin, just north
        of where The Wall made its turn.

Soldiers built The Wall—but where it was thinnest,
        didn't follow the plans—cut a plot of land

clean off the face of East Berlin. Created a neutral zone,
        untouchable, in West Berlin. There,

on passage O, at the border of Mitte, a Turkish migrant,
        Osman, planted on a property pronounced derelict—

cultivated apple trees and peach trees and alliums. He gifted
        guards in the watchtower with onions—

fed soldiers in the East and West. How he flustered,
        pleasured both sides. *The Lion* is what they called him.

In photographs, he smiles with his mouth open. Wears
        a long beard, slippers, and a coarse-woven cardigan.

In stories, he works—he carries onions, like babies, slung
        in a shawl, each week to market.

His granddaughter Funda swears this is why he lived
        so long—no meal could be begun, he wouldn't

taste a single morsel
        unless onions were on the table.

Learning the Art of Regifting

Grandfather wielded a right-angled ruler, two planks
the length of my arms, pointed in multiple directions
at all times. A folding wooden baton. He stored it
deep in the pocket of his Dickies—always at hand.
He must have used it to build his workshop: walls
of wooden blocks, a roof of rectangles and squares,
loft stacked with rows of stained-glass jars,
windows high and narrow on the garage door.
But I only saw him use the ruler to wrap gifts for family
parties, celebrations where people ate from piles of fresh
fruit and crustless finger sandwiches.
I would stand at attention as he muttered incantations,
marked, bent paper to wrap the box in fat blossoms,
a gold-lined smattering on a flat background.
I never minded when it was his time,
when he sat with his gifts, turning them in his hands,
inspecting the seams with his fingertips to locate the tape
to cut with his pocketknife—without tearing the precious
wrap. He would smooth the blank interior, before
gently folding the paper and setting it aside until later—
when he would show me how it could hold a present
for someone else.

~ for AJM

To Build a Fire

I turn back

        to a library

            of specters gathered behind me. Say nothing

                    as I dismantle

a towering pile; strip hardbacks of their pages; with razor precision,
tear each sheet into slivers; create a bird nest of tinder; add

    sawdust.

        My desk transforms into a fireboard; the utensil in
    my hand, a spindle—a pressure drill to turn, transform
    softwood into hot fibers.

        There is no wasting time.   No rush.

  I keep up the back-and-forth, the twirling, until friction forms a
glowing ember-egg, which I tip into the nest.

             My long breath enters, releases
        whispers of smoke.

The first layer ascends in a flash of blue electric; the second, a flurry
of blistering ink; the third, a whirl of plucked feathers,
fallen needles, and dandelion fluff.

    We all pitch in to the fire.

The room crackles and darkens. With the ash-black tip of my spindle,
I draw a line from the billowing hearth to the door

◊
◊
◊

In Darkness: The Harbor (1817)

Regenerate what has fallen: rise
        with the river, each spring,

where knees reach skyward
        in supplication to the black

sky, star
        punctuated, perforated

darkness, behind
        the curtain of light

at the bend
        in the river,

as a miracle is simple
        as a shoulder at your side,

a full cup in hand, and plenty
        is a memory of having

neither want nor need,
        only joy as the water

climbs
        the levee

and our mothers' seeds call
        for planting, to sprawl

like banquettes sprouting
        from the apothecary door.

~ for AR

The Ballad of Double D

When Double D returned the first time, he arrived
at our Christmas party, a brand-new man—
an incarnation, shiny as the six-inch buckle
twanging below his banded Stetson.

His boots, too, were made of skin, and curved
faintly toward the popcorn ceiling—
the fool, he was in Ruston, trading in his
training in controlled flight—pilot lessons—

for trailer life, coupon-clipping, square
cubes floating on four fingers of bourbon.
His lover'd given him a real fancy accent.
And yea you bet she sure could cook good—

oven brisket bbq, no boxed macaroni,
fresh corn on the cob—all that butter his mama
wouldn't let him eat straight from the tub.
But her baby wasn't his, and country was never suited for

jazzy sax, electric guitar—his first love,
native tongue—the home that followed him
on the road, leather repelling the open
heavens, rubber gripping hot to the highway

to show hipsters in Saint Louis how he'd play
their instruments if he were them.
Had to trade it all in
exactly like the van that broke down

on that last trip, cuz
maybe the condom broke and maybe it didn't
but the Mandeville rich still practice shotgun weddings
even if the man is of such low stock

he's never seen a blanket ladder—after all,
working class works—so he worked for her:
credit cards and indentured servitude
for a mortgage her father paid.

He toiled.
He teetered for a decade.
She got four degrees, four kids, alimony.
He got time. He got free.

He also got a TikTok account, a room
at his parents' place in Picayune, and a 12-gauge
ear piercing—a silver hoop. This time,
he showed up on my front porch, Black

Friday, with a steel-stringed acoustic, soul
patch, and a bottle of peanut butter whiskey.
We were playing UNO like our elders once did—
circled around the dining room table,

smoking bud instead of tobacco,
when he gave thanks for enduring the incident—
the kind our Uncle Harry and cousin Leslie didn't.
I asked him

what made him, standing
at the lake's edge, decide
not to do it. He said I didn't—
the safety, inexplicably, was on.

He took that as a sign, saying
he was mistaken. He was alive.
He could still go home. I told him
I agreed.

How I knew.
How the dreamlife becomes dreamwalking.
How we rise, eyes open.
How we rise, breathing water.

~ for DMJ

Birthday Poem

In high school, we celebrated
our springtime birthdays
with cake and frozen daiquiris,
bbqs and crawfish boils. In college
we added Saint Paddy's Day parades,
chasing shots of Jameson with Mic Ultras,
sucking heads and catching heads of cabbage
hurled from floats rolling
down Annunciation Street.

◊

For this birthday, for a change
we meet halfway
for a dinner of surf-and-turf.
A bottle of spirits moors in your throat,
anchoring you with a generous berth,
as you silently crest and sink,
watching the shoreline
of the route we've mapped,
the docks where we have loaded
and unloaded again.

We travel between these river repasts,
each following our opposing banks,
the sun and moon rising and sinking
through zeniths and horizons,
but rarely over our heads,
before or behind us ...

◊

Our future may be past
the dead zone
of the river's mouth,
an eventual path—

maybe sticking to the coast,
ducking into bays with familiar names
to share
a plate of fried potatoes—

maybe searching for the remote
island beaches you favor,

      drifting
      over black fathoms, fishing

         far
         into the open Gulf.

         ~ for AC

After the Twister

7pm. 9th Ward March. Folk sup on porches.

Pops is behind bars.
Sis is out looking

      For parts to repair her shotgun double. In spite of the itch,
In spite of the burning swell, I'd like to stay outside,

        Among others' voices—

To count my blessings. Yes—blessings are what I might recall now
      Facing night's sun-rimmed ascent—in spite of my skin

Pricked by mosquitos, the empty church, the teeming police station
In my ear. Beside me. Behind me. Buzzing.

Blessed to porchsit.
Blessed by canta

-loupes dusking at my feet.
Blessed to sleep
          In a rented room.
          Blessed to remember I'm home

    -free, which is to be bound
    -less (a blessing, too) knowing I am nevertheless

      Blessed by the houses my kin built, their
Cracked stucco

Planked walls hiding
    Belongings—tilting land
      Shifting under concrete.
             Blessed as they
         Fall. As I am.

    ~ for SDN

Watching Uncle Pit's Place Burn

just out of sight of this stoop
the first house I remember still stands

house with a garden of cacti
sweet and fluffy to the eye
like rabbits caged in
Paw Paw's backyard

garden that stuck my hand
with a hundred needles
when I tried to touch it
when I thought I could hold it

house with a leaking ceiling that rained on
my molding toy room
house where I chipmunked aspirin
what I thought was candy

and the old remedy
the pharmacist's ipecac
made me wish for death
made it all come up

house that taught me
the ways of life in the form
of a peanut-butter snap-trapped mouse
I thought would be our pet

house with an attic full
of fire from which I was carried
across the street
in the arms of a stranger

where I was granted
a window view of my home's rescue
from my neighbors' bed

Dancing-School Queen

In the '80s, I pretended
our scuffed linoleum parquet
was a studio-stage. Tapped an L
through the living room and kitchen
before stepdad made me quit.
I didn't know what he meant—

what he said my body did.
How my size-three
shuffle ball change
made people think
about touching
my body.

How I provoked
his rage
against my body
as I passed
between his eyes
and the television screen.

I never stopped
but ended up
a front-lawn
cheerleader:
all angles,
a base

repeating
rhyming
ends.
By then
I knew
what he meant.

Candy Kid

2001. New Orleans. House of Blues.
SIN. Service Industry Night.
I was accustomed to second-lining,
walking in time,

always smiling but not showing my teeth.
The stage was above in front of me. I was in the pit.
Wide-legged pants. Red spaghetti tank. Vans.
Looking for the ladies' room, I wandered away from my friends.

Was suddenly surrounded. Six men shining, slick beautiful. Tried
to be cool but was frozen—wrists ankles cuffed body tossed
into air, onto one thrusting, the others pulling yanking, twisting
hips flailing, open mouths and teeth cackle and crackle. Static
in my ears.

In a flash I was set down. Feet on ground.
I weaved my way to the side door,
through the alley,
into the trafficked night.

2003. Chinatown.
DNB. Breakbeat Night.
I tried to pretend a narrow club in Manhattan
was just like State Palace—then the drugs kicked in.

My first rave may have been
backpacks, pony tails, and pixie sticks.
A little LSD. Colors motioning toward flow.
There was never enough water. When I left,

Riverboat Hallelujah's corridors towered
with teenagers: writhing arms, legs, and pacifiers.
I couldn't get out soon enough.
I remember driving.

This last time, four men followed me. See them
in my rearview: two to distract and slip the mickey;
two to attract and slip. Slick.
I drove off, but then ... I forget.

Lucky is a single Long Island iced tea, good instincts,
and coming to, alive in Brooklyn. Reflectors on the turnpike
tearing open the door of my new Focus,
waking me from my sleep.

Last Carnival's Dramedy

So there.

Now we woke up—and the sun says through his teeth *why don't you paint a star, a glacier-colored 5-point under your eye.* But why listen to that guy waggling his eyebrows —he's just trying to sell rainbows, tomorrow—though I have to admit his lipstick is the slickest, richest, most even and durable shade I've ever seen; and the clouds that come with the rainbows are pretty?

He says *you're the moon, what do you know about clouds,* and Earth starts crying cuz she can't see her clouds like we do— and I would reach out if I had limbs but I don't and neither does that creep the sun who wants to draw us closer with his candy land.

He'll burn us up.

But I'm cool and you're certainly not frozen. I say *put on your purple coat, gold collar.* You say *why don't we take a picture instead?* Yes! I will hold your sickle while you take that cheesy cape off your shoulders—

O! can you see how we'll see the sun, as he retreats, sinks, dipping low in a sky of hibiscus tea to sip from my new-moon chalice, as I am tipping back, to wash his glitter, his watercolor dust, from our hands?

~ for RM

Return to Thunder Rock

having found myself
        bleeding, offering to what swarmed
                the stinking vaulted pit—found empty

tuna cans, condoms, wraps
        where I'd thought to build a fire—
                I took the Secret Crick—

a lip-locked sliver prying mountain's gritty fold—
        I had to drag—drag down the mountain
                to its twice-told shore—to the edge

of the seedy maypop wild—listening
        slept on splintered ground—when I woke
                I heard

how Ocoee whispered instead of roared—
        how the copperhead, how little beauty,
                how the meadow bowed.

This
        was where
                the river broke—

by the dam, the bridge
        I'd crossed in the tented pitch.
                I then slipped

on my handsewn skirt
        of ivory and sunset and lapis lazuli
                and crossed the tributary by foot.

           ~ for BC

Dandies, Wilde

~ after Robin Coste Lewis's "The Wilde Woman of Aiken"

You cannot prevent us / from casting sun / flowers to seed
at the fence (hedging / a border trap / crop for diamond

backed stink / bugs) purple mustard / greens thick
unruly at our feet / sheltering snail / orgies of orange leaf

footed nymphs / are welcomed / we cast
your brocades aside / slip shoes off / at the door

dig the clay / deep / where the water
table rises / spin earth / -en vessels

our voices are / sitting in / the open
glow of swelling / night / shades in rows

keep your corn / keep your measures / this spring
you'll find / only / broken

vases and gates / flung rusted / against your march
may we weave / the dried invasives / under no one's

watchful eye / fill them / with eager
with spicy radish / harbored by / pickling

cucumber vine / okra welcoming / the sugar
ants to our west / a million / underfoot

we don't bury our dead / we house them / behind welded
iron curling / still listening / dark

welcomes / what has always / existed
you try / try try / but you

can never / stamp / our abundance

~ for CH

Before the Storm

After moving—ever closer—since I saw her first
hawking the London Canal (next cracking open
the shell of an apple snail on the ladder breaching
the levee between my dwelling and the waterway)
today—today the wind has its way—she lands
headfirst bucking on the wood fence above my
patch of pea sprouts black worm flat dangling long
from her sharp hook her closed beak and our eyes meet
for a moment—she is magnificent—a full foot of brilliant
colors of sunrise or sunset, moth eyes camouflaged
blink from her tail feathers as the wind
has its way we see—equally clearly—each other
for a moment before she is tossed disappearing
into the howl of storm echoing today's sky.

~ for KDW

Song for Myself

as I was born spacious
sprung from sunshine

glimpse my hailing image

my shield
is crested

ore mined   charcoal pressed
towers loomed and looming

as does the horizon—
nevertheless   I cross

where your gripping fingers
where your thumbs hook

I slouch up your ladder with my gospel
crawl into your stable door

Solstice Ritual With My First-Born

~ after Tori Green's series The Wild Woman Is Unkempt

At Cricket's Gift Horst, the wild
woman, unkempt, levers loose

the teeth in my ears. *"Mola, Mulyana,"*
she shrugs. Places them in your mouth.

Her eyes are all antennae and leafy moth wings.
She sinks her fingertips into her sternum and pries

her chest apart, releasing bees in a ribbon
from the cavity that that was her body.

Why hadn't I noticed the honeycomb above her antlered head?
My hand signs *thank you*, and we walk our way. You wear

two green stones, bezel-set, in skyscraper pendulums
dangling like lanky pears in pirouette.

The entrance is dark, but you wear a headlamp.
I am breathless, but you laugh and shimmy closer,

show me the empty cup of your palm
as you whisper *she made it by hand.*

Silver-eyed, I see you for the first time:
Your body is not attached

to your head is not attached
to your—My head

is not attached.
We say, "Yes."

~ for TG

Cute, Joyce ...

~ after "Where Are You Going, Where Have You Been"

'cept you got it all wrong. I was the one
stuffing my tits lumpy with tissues, standing

on tippy toes—and there
weren't no such thing as pre

-meditating involved
when he showed up,

no baggage, driving
not a convertible but a Durango

and I happened to be
headed to Durango.

Road signs. Yet we both got tongue-
tied-up until I slowslank and no-looking

-back led him to the field—to where
my folks will never find us, though they love

the hunt. I imagine they pushed
the vehicle we abandoned

into a pond before rounding up
some other poor goat, some other

outcast; and broadcasted his smooth eye
-lined bewilder, to blame; then made up

another story to tell
about me.

~ for NU

Ariadne and Hippolyta Dialogue on Exes

During the break. In scene. When he says he
"Just. Can't look. At those Tentacled Eggs."

        Call it quits. Dig the dark
        Lengthened shadow.

From the start. The first clew. What we knew
He desired. Gold-smelt finger-coils. Helixed. Our

        Form. As a butterfly hairpin. To carry. A tiny
        Glow. A twilight. In his pocket.

Don't you know he always
Makes good offerings. Ceremonies

        In my name. A horse. Remember
        The girdle. How to let it loose.

How he escaped with it. What he
Himself needed. What he

        Thought. What he
Wanted to wear.

All Theseus Ever Wanted: An Heir

Me? a fearsome daughter of Otrera, of Ares ... my quiver is as hungry as his. On my island his siring would be weaned and left cold in the green peaks 'tween our kind and his—only meeting where and when we've agreed. I never. I never imagined I would ever see such moonless spring as on the night they shuffled me—*ducere*—*seducere*. Even his tongue won't pronounce what he meant. What he means. Now we cross a gulf with him fathering fathers—where murky translation is a familiar reason for his aggressive tangle. While our child gestates. Where I persist.

~ *for KM*

Ariadne's Side

At the leap-dance, I was his vision—
a pinch-face lily, a gypsum cliff.

He'll say my voice was a lantern,
claim my hair was a skein—

a twisted yarn, divined,
just for him.

Theseus woke dreaming of the cave
but discovered the ceiling missing

miles above the flickering
of hearth ash cold

cascading from my skin—
the same constellations.

Here, I take form as clay, and this land—
Dia—is my reason. My seal is

stained glass—arisen
liber of flesh washed ashore.

Walls and games aside
in this wild, I'll stay.

Theseus wanted dolphins painted
on the labyrinth floor—a good end.

Slip-knotted to his bark, he follows
his father's routes

so he flew, black sails
facing the wrong direction.

~for BR

After She Escaped the Labyrinth

Calliste's pumice walls quaked—
collapsed: a pyroclastic
cloud-crowned farewell to lustral

basins and vibrant orant
poses. Beeswaxed trunks, buried
to bedrock, shock absorbed all

that remains—what is known. Their
once-elite bodies trained to
dance, to retire, were

lost under epiphany
fire. In their time, divine
appeared

in any form: Fishermen
painted on every surface—
frescoes, woven agora—

drank from the mouths of bovine
horns in Egyptian gold. They
forgot the wine, olive oil

once was blood. Islanders knew
no empty places—filled gaps
in wooden walls with pebbles—

filled gaps in wooden planks with
plaster—built rooms that flexed. She
forgot every sacrifice.

~ *for MAN*

The River Merchant's Wife

a letter from Petit Jean, Arkansas

Your hanging
edge of marigolds has
disintegrated, piling petals
that billow like a flame congealed by
the door. I found my keys in the surge beneath
your empty patio pachyderm's cadmium-laced heartbeak.

So long since

your skiff skimmed scales, held

down my hem and departed,

hunting
the globe for
bleached coral

lobes, sashimi'ed Buddha bowls, sugared
cake crumbs for your tongue—
when I woke I walked
circles under your vaulted ceilings, cobbled
stone cold against
bare feet.
You stay gone.
Now I know the buoyancy of water

drop wings, fins
that steer me
far away
upstream for days
divided by half
and half and half.

While you skirt hollows, know I coast. I climb. I traipse
whorled bluffs of turtles' backs.

~ for MT

53

Fresh From the Apothecary (2023)

I'll drop in unannounced, like there is no time—

as time is of no consequence, as in I'm here and who needs a
name or a plan—for going home is the way home—back toward
what will be and is now Canal Street, back toward the original
neutral ground.

I'll break the story as I please, rip it at the seams, use the thread
to tie my hair in a tangle, punctuated with an egret's feather,
satsuma blossom, cypress sprig.

I'll shoulder a chair by the fire, hover by the door, catch a drift, ride a
wake of conversation or a draft of business, equations, a street full

of tourists, checking in on Google, TikTok, selfie sticks in fists,
pockets full of credit, at this ancient crossroad, port, drawing
upon people from afar, mainlining

by river, leap-frogging to steamrolling to internal combustion
driving upstream like so many salmon to empty themselves, in
exchange, for such pleasures.

I'll thresh the harvest where the whim takes me, where it takes
hold, casting both hull and seed windward as I like,

no superimposed division between what belongs to the belly,
grave, or sky, as earth I'll shake and swallow everything whole.

What you can count on: I'll end the song

when I—the feeling strikes me, drop the shoe, drop my hat, drop
a word, a line over a heartbeat—

a drop of bitters, as a Haitian elixir, for the mouthfeel. For the
finish.

~ for SB

At NOMA: Do Not Climb the Sculpture

~after Robert Graham's Source Figure

to rise
           from <u>water</u>—once
           a bridge parting
           water—what now is

a petrified pool a chromium wave suspended

...

refugee
among wired oaks
bronzed thighs

                     naked—
                     reposed—*reposta*

atop a barnacled
                column by
                        snap of dungeness
                        crabs guarded

...

cupped hands hold
                    the cap of
                an acorn—sprouts and burrows
                                         crack
the marble pedestal
                              under cast feet

           ~ for JA

On Paul Gauguin and Musée d'Orsay

I'd rather linger among the small bodies—
Venuses that passed us the stones' ages

under full moons. They gathered
wheat, kept our bearings, headed

home. What the painting covets:
to be seen—

to beget
an italicized name—

to be auctioned at the banks of the Seine.
How the French imagined. Above:

layers of terracotta pink,
green banana leaf. Below:

reapers sleep and tedders dream.
These memories work

both ways—as gathered frames.
Toulouse remains up top, with Monet;

Bastien-Lepage's *Les Foins*
in the basement hallway, with me.

~ *for ARS*

Climbing Mutspitze in Tirolo

                              nordic lift to corn
                    -hanging christ
                  -stabled crossroad

stone-stack offerings
        to madonnas
                in canopy-alcoves

falling glass
        trickling rush
                from glacier lake above

...

        sometimes trees are cathedrals—narrow
        halls, buttressed

        sometimes forests open to tilted balds—

                cool runways

                                for rising

    our bodies make temporary stencils

...

as sun sets at the hostel
                we continue on, silence

                close
                behind us
                        as night settles and
                mountain's stony soilglow pulses
        from evergreens'
                springing carpet

I envision tomorrow's panorama clearly
collaged—super-imposed—my teeth

show my tongue
when I smile
my body is seamed
polygons white
-shirt wet eyes

diverted
to stone
to great mother
mountain

who knows the time (who knows where we are) is

navigating shadows
planting feet
in the light
river to the left
between wind
whisper cut trunks
faint globe
of city asleep
lifts ahead
from valley
below
we follow
the river song's
promise of
the sky parting
at dawn

we'll wash our hiking sandals where the distant tributary ends,
where watershed wears bridges, birches, and sloping levee parks,
where water widens—where water splits

the old city from the new

Practicing off the Coast of the Lido

The Adriatic lulls and contracts—
a double ouroboros
        of gold
            freckled jade.
                        I drift
past the shelled blockade.
    Let wakes sheath my body.
                My hair is spun brass threads
            catching light—a crown of glass
        snakes, writing adagio notes.
        Eyes fixed on a bulb-nosed
                        buoy, head
hanging bright in air.

Water never swallows me whole.
            I am *port de bras* arms
                pointed foot and toe
                    passé, retiré
            connecting before
        I press my sole flat
                to my inner
            thigh—

            Pivoting Crane!
        In this pitching
                the sea holds me
            afloat.

~ *for HM*

Other Dawns

rooster
crows

silver
slivers

the violet Sky's
quiet

we don't just
walk our way

with crane
-legs

arms back
-bounded

we hang
blindfolded

plant-rooted

nebulae

~for JWN

From the Mountains, From the Island, From Desert Storms—I Returned

Done with trekking, I recall
my razed neighborhood—

that scatter of concrete foundations—
their footprints in right angles

where wood studs molded,
leaving smutty marks.

> The flood waters have long receded.
> I envision our summers—

how our curtains would lift
and fall,

how I folded linens
into creases,

how I swept myself up in star
-dazing. How my passion

was to be always
chatter-walking.

How I'd had to turn back to face
it all. My obsession. My desire.

Café au Lait on the Moonwalk

Our mornings welcome
the undercurrent

from the surface,
what flows, what drags

our leap-frog progression: the ports'
steam-roller locomotions.

When you laugh, I recall how
even in the wine-dark,

hull deep in the river,
your eyes flash and flutter,

sails catching wind,
blinking a Morse code.

~ *for EB*

Creole Recipe Card for Nonviolence

6 carrots, 10 baby bellas, half of a half of a head
of cabbage, a handful of eggs, scarce, to fry
with basmati and quinoa hailing
from lands oceans apart in
hot sunflower oil spiced
with house-made roasted
garlic roasted
homegrown serrano
red pepper red
wine fresh oregano leaf
in olive oil pulverized
in two large dollops finished
with liquid aminos and coconut oil.   Days grow
longer.   Xmas tree's still standing—
          white light   now multicolored   for the gras.
Last night's dinner was raisins, chocolate chips, honeyed O's.
For breakfast—only coffee.
All fair trade.

                    One recipe
I didn't inherit from my family—soup
                                        from alligator snapping
                              turtle, beheaded, cuz
              after my uncle was crunched under duct
work industrial on the river, Maw Maw lost her hair
and she swore she would never kill again.

          ~ for AMJ

The Last

~after Irván "Pooka" Pérez

The elders—versed in measured tides,
in wine-red gulfs, traditions—
exaggerate their trappings
every hurricane season

at the end of the world. Smitten
with nursery rhymes and riddles,
Pooka insists his décimas be read
as if we've never read before ...

       His cans shake—as it was said—he
       shakes his cans.
...

No. Wrong tense.

His pale quaked—as it is said—
       he shook his pail.

Scales can shake all he sang
from his quaking mail. His chains. His trade
was delivering songs to kings.

He trawled our decades for decades
to collect our Islander names
in docu-pigeon sound-strains. Look—

strain sounds like a man
honin' a decoy. A carved block.
A duck.

   ...

       True. Betsy blew down the great dance hall.

Still—even after the last big storm—it'll take never
for the dead to settle down.

A Round (of Ends and Beginnings)

"Ezra Pound, Yusef Komunyakaa, and Billy Collins walk into a bar,"
he thought aloud, presuming to formulate a joke.

A photo gallery looms behind him, a pantheon of writers
posing for the cameraman, and I can't help but laugh out loud
in response to

such a preposterous premise—and how such a beginning
and end is only possible in New Orleans, where cages, where
prison cells

transform into redolent landscapes, sunshine beaded verses,
fractured beauty, fractured memories, mania beating its wing

toward horizons. Where else other than this sinking city,
scored by banquettes marking a timely path to innumerable
destinations,

might the emperor, the warrior, and the teacher collide, empty
and fill their cups, and with humor consider the similarities

between a rubber hose, a wall, and a dwelling composed of
bars? Only muddy water bounds past the rocky levee

here, where the under tows. Men line up to dine
at Napoleon's house, which was never a home.

Men line up to take a taste of a name, status,
traditions tagged on menus.

Keep walking.
To our east is the west, the opposing bank,

where sojourners seek open airs, reflections on currents,
where Calliope busts her pipes, an angel's or a siren's song,
distant.

See how close we may approach the water's edge
without being swept downstream, dragged down

to the dead zone of the river's destination,
where life is blind,

where life withstands shell-smashing pressure,
the weight of an entire world.

~ for KO

Transmission From αCMa

Whether you are Chaldea—or over those deserts, Egypt—
glimpse us beside the Milky Way alight. Within our wobbling
orbit, we're rerouting age-old myths. Quiet, fire hot.

We've known the swell of bliss—eclipsed our Sirius B.
Cygnus made a love called Supernova—a mortal rendered her
Eve. Don't we like to think

we float beyond such scorched horizons—but we grasp
mere reflections for sight. Know this—globes will frizzle
as we are gathering worlds. After all

stones are small and sinking. Children conceive positions,
the heavens—assign names, imagining fixed systems—

                                        nevertheless
                    we draw
near from far

and though this song will end, we mash with Sol, twist
circles round Luna, and tap a Terrestrial tango—
ever after.

Altar :: Objects

The hutch of my great-grandfather's secretary desk
is littered by a girl on the move:

a collection of projections of her heading
in the direction of womanhood. It might be called

the way I am bound to be bounded
by concrete objects, to memory bright and fast,

altered by additions: the twig brought home
by my child (an alligator is what he saw—

beady eyes, long snout peeping from bayou water);
a gift from a stranger in Hilo who, after I

listened to his folk stories, placed a clipped lobe of
coral in my hands, when I had to go;

two crisscrossed loofa sponges, cellulose skeletons
mistaken for sea creatures in their afterlife, but in life going

in all directions, a prolific vine, filling
gaps in my Arabi chain-link, before my move,

with bitter-skinned babies, providing shady cool;
a trio of ceramic owls, added to a collection I

never intended, the see-no-hear-no-speak-no-evil totems
I tote; the chalky oyster shell I saw

underfoot while I led my daughter, dancing, in her first parade;
a seed of what's called

by many names (marshmallow, wild hibiscus, swamp rose), good
for migrating birds, for healing faster,

for growing beautiful in dark, dank places deemed inhospitable;
a sliver of a tree that held fast

to the Mississippi's ancient path, a cypress
buried, preserved for 2,000 years in a crevasse now gone,

no longer necessary as the levee keeps the river
in its place; a collage on a piece of sawed-

off 1x4, magazine-clipped words across forests, black
cherry magenta, deep ocean teal, moving

acrylic splashes and swirls, and a single tuft of wolf
lichen, lime-green fluorescent; a candle I recall

was labelled *Man Cave*, amber beeswax that refused
to continue burning, that I

set aflame over and over, to no end; a scatter of
purple, green, and gold doubloons I

snatched from the air, a pelting
precipitation that my fast

thinking stopped from wounding the children
in Lafayette Square, aluminum faces *kalli-*

graphia-embossed with the old gods' names; a hand-
cast shoji white teapot, no cups to go

with it, bone-dry unsealed ceramic, never filled, forever
silent; a smooth sienna rock removed

from the North Umpqua River, where I planted
my feet, wildfire around me, and I saw

how pines are renewed; the empty shell of a garden
snail reminding me of the old saw

by Donne, any who *doth roam, carrying their own house
still, still is at home*, which I

found, delicate and intact on the floor
of my first studio apartment, when I finally moved

out, on my own; a speck of burnt granite I plucked
while contemplating my fast

life, thusly lightning-struck, from the highest point
of Summerville Trail, and I chose to go

back, down to the Wild below Fossil Ridge, giving
into my hunger for sound, the call

of water falling into the valley; the birthday
candle, dedicated to my calling,

my first manuscript, the candle that finally lit
the wick of that stubborn *Man Cave*, which I saw

and continue to see, as lighting the path before me;
an unfinished quartz, aplite-veined, that goes

with the relics I gathered on my trip
westward and home again, stone durable as I

hope to be, electric under pressure, thermal shock
resistant, what our ancestors learned to fasten

to wooden shafts as hammerstones, to make choppers,
to craft instruments for moving,

bending air, music from flutes carved from bone; my grandmother's
Tiffany lamp, bronze–based, what I

inherited, an illuminated circle of dragonflies in emerald,
cobalt, and crimson glass, descending fast

though never landing on this altar, perching
above me while I write, following my every move.

~ for MRN

Notes

αCM: Also referred to as αCanis Major, Alpha Canis Major, the Dog Star; Sirius is the brightest star in the night sky, part of a triple-star system previously seen as one.

Banquette: A term used through the 20th century, it originally referred to the early sidewalks of New Orleans' Vieux Carré (now the French Quarter), built from "barge board," or lumber from the dismantled flatboats that delivered people and goods to the city; because they were raised to keep foot traffic above its muddy, flooded streets, they resembled elevated benches, hence the name.

Betsy: We are on a first-name basis with hurricanes in New Orleans. 50 years before Katrina, Betsy—a category 4 storm— blew into town, breaking the levees in the 9th Ward, flooding our families' homes, and leaving a wake of death in her path and our collective memory.

Calliste: Translated from Greek, the name means most beautiful; also called Thera, this volcano-island erupted, obliterating its inhabitants and causing the tsunami that also destroyed the entire island of Crete, including the palace at Knossos—the Labyrinth.

Creole has a complex history that requires more than a glossary entry to gloss; suffice to say that while what might be labeled a Creole tomato is a subject of controversy, most agree that it is the soil itself at the mouth of the Mississippi that makes a tomato Creole, imparting a flavor like no other.

"Dandies, Wilde": Robin Coste Lewis's ekphrastic, feminist and postcolonial/anti-colonial poem "The Wilde Woman of Aiken" (*The Voyage of the Sable Venus*, 2015) aims to empower the Black female figure in James A. Palmer's racist 1882 photograph by the same name. Palmer's photograph is a parody of "The Aesthetic Monkey," a homophobic cartoon, satirizing Oscar Wilde, which was also published in 1882, by *Harper's Daily*. See Victoria Daily's essay "The Wilde Woman and the Sunflower Apostle" (*Los Angeles Review of Books*, 2020).

Décima: Originating in medieval Spain, these songs open with a four-line refrain, followed by four ten-line stanzas; usually written with a regular rhyme scheme, in octosyllabics; lyrical or satirical; improvised or inherited; sung solo or in rounds. Décima singing is still practiced in Ecuador, Puerto Rico, and Peru.

Delacroix Island: Also referred to as The Island; Delacroix, Louisiana, was a fishing village established in the 1770s by Spanish immigrants from the Canary Islands, who identify as Isleños, or Islanders.

Down the Road: refers to any place south/southeast of the Violet Canal in St. Bernard Parish (originally part of New Orleans).

The End of the World: the southern limit of Delacroix Island, as prominently displayed by a sign where Louisiana Highway 300 (Delacroix Highway) ended its trek along Bayou Terre aux Boeuf.

The Great Dance Hall: Decimated by Hurricane Betsy in 1965, it was the only remaining cultural relic of a time when Isleños gathered on Saturday nights. Bands from New Orleans would perform until midnight, when everyone sat down for a grand repast of traditional foods, such as caldos, paella, and stuffed mirliton. Everyone stayed well past dinner, for that's when the décimeros began singing.

"I Am Who We Are": A translation of the Italian phrase *Io chi siamo*, the saying comes from *The Hundred Languages of Children* (1998), the seminal work on child-centered Reggio-Emilian education (in symbolic expression, as opposed to focusing on one spoken language, rote memorization, or rigid and hierarchized literacies).

In Darkness: The Harbor (1817): Antoinette Eulalis Rieux, an ancestor whose name I bear, was born this year. Her grandfather, L. Simon Rieux, a chemist and pharmacist, opened and operated the apothecary located at 37 Toulouse Street.

Lido: Also referred to as The Lido; Lido di Venezia, Italy, is a village on a barrier island separating the central portion of the Venice Lagoon from the Adriatic Sea.

The Moonwalk: is a pedestrian path, stretching alongside the Mississippi River, from one end of the French Quarter to the other; moving up-river, it begins at the French Market and passes Café du Monde and St. Louis Cathedral before ending on Canal Street, at the Aquarium of the Americas.

Mutspitze: translated from German, means great courage; also called Monte Muta, this mountain in the South Tyrol region of Italy was part of Austria before World War I; its summit trail leads to the Spronser Lakes, left behind by glaciers, the most massive collection of their kind in the Alps.

Neutral Ground: *The Picayune* in New Orleans coined the term in 1837, when they used it to refer to the median on Canal Street, which then separated two distinct (rival) cultural districts—with Creoles to the east and Anglo-Americans to the west; now, neutral ground is vernacular for any grassy median separating lanes of opposing traffic on a divided highway in Greater New Orleans.

Pigeon: (also pidgin) refers to a regionally specific language combining the vocabularies and syntaxes of two or more languages.

Thunder Rock: is a campground on the Ocoee River, on Forest Service Road 45, just off U.S. Highway 64 and behind Powerhouse Number 3, in the Cherokee National Forest, Copperhill, Tennessee.

"To Build a Fire": A whole vocabulary exists to name the tools, means, and methods used to accomplish said task without a match or lighter: a bark, baseboard, fireboard, spindle, bearing block, a rock, bow, groove, plough, wood dust, branches, beeswax, pine pitch, rolling, repeating, ember, oil from your hair or skin, a parachute cord, rope, shoelace, leather thong, tinder bundle, ember catch, breath, rhythm, touch, sound, sight, maximum speed, pressure, caution, a nest, tinder shavings, kindling and the like, and so on and so on.

About the Author

M.A. Nicholson is a New Orleans poet, editor, and educator whose critical writing appears in *Diode Poetry Journal*, *New Orleans Review*, and elsewhere. An alumna of Loyola University and a M.F.A. graduate from the University of New Orleans—where she served as Associate Poetry Editor for *Bayou Magazine*—M.A. was the recipient of the 2021 Andrea-Saunders Gereighty Academy of American Poets Award and is a co-founder of LMNL Arts, a nonprofit dedicated to supporting writers and fostering community through readings, workshops, festivals, anthologies, and more. Connect with M.A. at michellenicholsonpoetry.com.

About the Artist

Tori Green is a multidisciplinary designer and native to New Orleans, LA. Her work explores how people interact with and within natural and constructed environments. She specializes in creating immersive experiences, multimedia graphics, and illustrations for museums, exhibits, events, and installations globally. She developed a love for both design and the discipline's history at the Kansas City Art Institute, where she received BFAs in Graphic Design and Art History. All her projects are narrative-based and combine storytelling with visuals to create experiences that engage, inform, surprise, and delight people from all walks of life. Her most recent experiential design collaborations have been with Google, YouTube, TikTok, Niantic, Pfizer, and Meta.

About The Word Works

Since its founding in 1974, The Word Works has steadily published volumes of contemporary poetry and presented public programs. Its imprints include The Washington Prize, The Tenth Gate Prize, The Hilary Tham Capital Collection, and International Editions.

Monthly, The Word Works offers free programs in its Café Muse Literary Salon. Starting in 2023, the winners of the Jacklyn Potter Young Poets Competition will be presented in the June Café Muse program.

As a 501(c)3 organization, The Word Works has received awards from the National Endowment for the Arts, the National Endowment for the Humanities, the D.C. Commission on the Arts & Humanities, the Witter Bynner Foundation, Poets & Writers, The Writer's Center, Bell Atlantic, the David G. Taft Foundation, and others, including many generous private patrons.

An archive of artistic and administrative materials in the Washington Writing Archive is housed in the George Washington University Gelman Library. The Word Works is a member of the Community of Literary Magazines and Presses.

wordworksbooks.org

Books in the Hilary Tham Capital Collection

Nathalie Anderson, *Stain*
Mel Belin, *Flesh That Was Chrysalis*
Carrie Bennett, *The Land Is a Painted Thing*
Tara Betts, *Refuse to Disappear*
Doris Brody, *Judging the Distance*
Sarah Browning, *Whiskey in the Garden of Eden*
Grace Cavalieri, *Pinecrest Rest Haven*
Nikia Chaney, *to stir &*
Cheryl Clarke, *By My Precise Haircut*
Christopher Conlon, *Gilbert and Garbo in Love*
       &   Mary Falls: Requiem for Mrs. Surratt
Donna Denizé, *Broken Like Job*
W. Perry Epes, *Nothing Happened*
David Eye, *Seed*
Bernadette Geyer, *The Scabbard of Her Throat*
Elizabeth Gross, *this body / that lightning show*
Barbara G. S. Hagerty, *Twinzilla*
Lisa Hase-Jackson, *Flint & Fire*
James Hopkins, *Eight Pale Women*
Donald Illich, *Chance Bodies*
Brandon Johnson, *Love's Skin*
Ed Madden, *A pooka in Arkansas*
Thomas March, *Aftermath*
Marilyn McCabe, *Perpetual Motion*
Judith McCombs, *The Habit of Fire*
James McEwen, *Snake Country*
Kevin McLellan, *in other words, you/*
Miles David Moore, *The Bears of Paris*
       &   Rollercoaster
Kathi Morrison-Taylor, *By the Nest*
M. A. Nicholson, *Around the Gate*
Tera Vale Ragan, *Reading the Ground*
Michael Shaffner, *The Good Opinion of Squirrels*
David Allen Sullivan, *Black Butterflies Over Baghdad*
Maria Terrone, *The Bodies We Were Loaned*

Hilary Tham, *Bad Names for Women*
     & *Counting*
Barbara Ungar, *Charlotte Brontë, You Ruined My Life*
     & *Immortal Medusa*
Jonathan Vaile, *Blue Cowboy*
Rosemary Winslow, *Green Bodies*
Kathleen Winter, *Transformer*
Michele Wolf, *Immersion*
Joe Zealberg, *Covalence*

Printed in the USA
CPSIA information can be obtained
at www.ICGtesting.com
JSHW020030260624
65391JS00005B/140